SWEET TEA

SWEET TEA

⊰ A PLAY ⊱

E. PATRICK JOHNSON

Foreword by Jane M. Saks

NORTHWESTERN UNIVERSITY PRESS

EVANSTON, ILLINOIS

Northwestern University Press
www.nupress.northwestern.edu

Printed in the United States of America

10 9 8 7 6 5 4 3 2 1

LIBRARY OF CONGRESS
CATALOGING-IN-PUBLICATION DATA

Names: Johnson, E. Patrick, 1967– author. | Saks, Jane M., writer of foreword.
Title: Sweet tea : a play / E. Patrick Johnson ; foreword by Jane M Saks.
Other titles: Sweet tea (Play)
Description: Evanston : Northwestern University Press, 2020.
Identifiers: LCCN 2020016974 | ISBN 9780810142404 (paperback) | ISBN 9780810142411 (ebook)
Subjects: LCSH: African American gay men—Southern States—Drama. | Gay rights—Southern States—Drama. | Homosexuality—Religious aspects—Drama. | Homophobia—Southern States—Drama. | African Americans—Attitudes—Drama. | Southern States—Social conditions—Drama.
Classification: LCC PS3610.O339 S94 2020 | DDC 812.6—dc23
LC record available at https://lccn.loc.gov/2020016974

In memory of George Eagerson (aka "Countess Vivian"),
Harold Mays, and David Candler (aka "D.C.")

CONTENTS

Foreword by Jane M. Saks *ix*

Preface by E. Patrick Johnson *xv*

Production History *xvii*

Sweet Tea 1

FOREWORD

Jane M. Saks

I play the tenor saxophone and I used to play with some remarkable men in their nineties on the South Side of Chicago. When I started learning from them I was in my late twenties.

We first met through a friend, and I asked if I could sit in the room and listen . . . just listen and watch. They said, "Jane, you have three strikes against you—you're female, you're Jewish, and you don't know how to play the horn." I said, "Other than that, I'm your girl!"

Over the twenty-five years of knowing and playing with them that ensued, they have taught me things I had felt before and assumed I understood, but they pushed me into deeper territory. Leon and Freddy, Elijah and James are longtime professional music men who played in Europe with the royalty of jazz. Because of segregation in the United States, here at home they performed only in clubs that would allow them and, of course, in their own clubs.

They allowed me to be myself while playing the horn and taught me how to be something else and how to collaborate. They taught me about the creative generosity that is necessary—essential—to most everything. When I played with them, I tried to blow myself boneless through the horn, leaving the inside incandescent. I tried to leave structure behind: to take only what enabled me to be something else and on my own terms at the same time as being part of a group. They enhanced my understanding of collaboration and creative and human transformation.

That is exactly what is was like working with E. Patrick to create our play *Sweet Tea* from his amazing, historic book.

I was the founding executive director of the Institute for the Study of Women and Gender in the Arts and Media, Columbia College Chicago. After some years of friendship and working together, I invited E. Patrick to be an artistic fellow at the institute. The invitation was to collaboratively develop a full theatrical play from his scholarly book. I shaped this opportunity to collaborate deeply with artists to create new work that broke boundaries, pushed artistic practices, shifted the so called "canon," and demanded risk, innovation, trust, and new narratives.

When I read the thousand-page manuscript—yes, I did—I realized the depth of the men of *Sweet Tea* and the man of Sweet Tea, E. Patrick, who spoke to them all. The complexity and diversity of experiences and hearts, the overlapping and related aspects of their lives and ours, became clear. Harold and Harold, Freddie, Duncan, Stephen, Chaz, C.C., and Countess Vivian. I fell in love and I stayed in love—with the men and with E. Patrick, his desire to know each human on their own terms with dignity and respect. I could feel and see that this could be an immersive experience of multiple dimensions. I wanted to see it live off the page, in something that would create larger audiences and create communal experiences beyond academia.

Through a two-year curated workshop process with incredible individuals—writers, performers, directors, music historians, thinkers—all the while, E. Patrick was writing, writing, writing as we worked to create the script of *Sweet Tea*, the play.

When I was quite young I had the honor of interviewing the extraordinary human and playwright August Wilson for a piece I was writing. Two hours into our conversation I asked him why theater, why not novels, poetry, musicals? He said, "I'm a black man in America. I know what it means for me to say to a group of people, mostly white people, you have to be here at 7 P.M., be quiet, sit down, in the dark, and listen to me and my people until I tell you it's time to go."

I thought to myself, it's about art, it's about power, and it happens in real time. I knew *Sweet Tea* was about art and power—about agency, authenticity of voice, sitting in the dark and the light of these men and E. Patrick blinding us all. It is about their spoken word out loud and uninterrupted.

As E. Patrick said, being an institute fellow, ". . . has changed the trajectory of my career as an artist and scholar. The fellowship program afforded me the opportunity to have an intensive workshop environment to develop my work that I have never had before. Jane's commitment to and investment in my work helped me see its potential beyond an insular academic community to imagine how it could impact the lives of people around the world."

Part of my work is to actually try to shift what is considered the mainstream canon. By adding to the historical record and forever changing who is counted and valued—who participates, has agency and who shows up. If we add to that canon and shift it, it is never the same.

If we start with the principle of human dignity, and trust it to lead us to art and justice, it leads us to many questions: Who isn't here? Who should be? What's missing? How could it be different? How could I be different in relationships with others? What isn't being asked, who isn't asking, and what method or strategy is not being used? These are the questions in creating the play. This is not about absence in terms of lacking, but the abundance of inclusion—the endless abundance of divergent experiences, perspectives, choices, and necessities. This makes the sweetest tea.

I can't talk about creating *Sweet Tea* the play without speaking about the theory and practice of creating queer space. The scholarship and engagement of queer space and all that comes with it is front of my mind always in my artistic practice and as I worked on *Sweet Tea* for all these years.

I think queer spaces are those that appropriate certain aspects of the material and social world in which we all live. Then they are composed into counter constructions to create the freer spaces of expression and resistance—less defined and less regulated spaces where we can be the other, on our own terms.

Some might say the queerest of all spaces is the void—the emptiness, the absence, the possibilities, the magic, the risks, the yet-to-be-filled or defined, the loss and the wild, borderless imagination. It offers a life orientation, larger than that already defined.

This void, too, E. Patrick brings to light, and we weave it through the play with poignancy and purpose. For example, through the making of the play, E. Patrick himself had to come to terms with his own relationship to the early HIV/AIDS crisis in the United States—the denial, loss, fear, longing, and regret.

These queer spaces and places are more ambivalent and porous and often more imaginative than the environments we negotiate every day. That is part of what I envisioned creating in *Sweet Tea* the play. It is the freedom of queerness and that freedom has liberty and a cost. However, it has the richness and risk that only emancipation can offer.

Thousands of people have now experienced this amazing work. We created countless opportunities for groundbreaking conversations across communities, populations, experiences, and geography. E. Patrick and the play received wonderful reviews and awards. During and after performances people came out to their families, cried, gasped, laughed, rallied, and swooned. Great performance is never the same, each night different in its own glory, pain, and mischief. In D.C. one night we had the audience flying from the rafters and E. Patrick hanging on for dear sweet tea life.

Of course, there were experiences all along the way: an earthquake (for real), hurricane (yes in D.C.), ice storm in Durham (first time in fifty years), back-stage peeing cups, dripping toxic glue from our glorious tree, current AIDS crisis deniers, almost blowing up the theater, older women falling in love with Patrick (including my mother, Queen Esther), twenty-four-hour toxic emergencies, racism, homophobia, hate mail and emails questioning motives, more craziness that cannot be mentioned, brilliance that beautifully blinded from every corner, personal triumphs, illness, loss, loss, more loss, tragedies, vulnerability, gorgeous surprises, gorgeous vulnerabilities, risk, mistakes, care, community, deep love, evolution, trust, fear, beauty, deep, love, and beauty . . . endless beauty. Always end with beauty.

But what I count as one of the most powerful impacts is that some members from the Library of Congress came to see the performances in D.C. They had begun an LGBT oral history project. *Sweet Tea* is part of it. I can say without a doubt that when gay black men of the South entered the library's halls swinging from the chandeliers—the Library of Congress was never to be the same again. That's changing the so-called canon.

What *Sweet Tea* the play does is add oxygen and audiences to *lives*—the men's lives and our own. Full Stop. These men will never stop. The stories always have oxygen if we tell them and listen for them . . . over and over and over again.

Sweet Tea Men always walk among us . . . here today . . . onward . . .

PREFACE

E. Patrick Johnson

Bearing witness to someone else's story is a gift. The *I* who tells and *eye* that witnesses create a life force both generative and holy— generative in the sense that the listener is often transported through time and space to places in his or her own mind through the other's tale. And holy in the sense that the consecration of mind, body, and soul in the moment of the story's telling makes it a thing divine.

Sweet Tea the book gathers the stories told to me in living rooms, kitchens, cafes, and on porches between two thick book covers. *Sweet Tea* the play gathers these same stories in my body. As Dwight Conquergood writes: "Opening and interpreting lives is very different from opening and closing books." Different, indeed. I am accountable in a new way now that these stories live inside me. In the transformation from page to stage I have become a diviner, a holder of truths that lie in the balance of life and death. These stories' *ashe* demands that they live in the universe.

The journey to crafting a play to hold stories this big was not easy, but with humility and fortitude I trudged forward. What emerged was not the story I wanted to tell, but the one the stories demanded—the ones my *body* demanded. Sweet tea does not always go down easy and many times does not quench your thirst. Sometimes it shocks your tongue, bitter from being brewed too long. Sometimes it leaves a slimy residue on the tongue from too much sugar. Sometimes it mugs you from behind, stealth in its alcoholic concealment. Sometimes it changes color right before your eyes. Sometimes it settles in your mouth and dissipates into thin air. Sometimes it just glows. No matter what, it is never as it seems.

My journey has not ended with this play, but in some ways has begun anew, especially now that these men have gracefully decided to join me. Now, I am both the *I* and the *eye*. And audience members have become yet another *eye*, but also an *I* as their own reveries and revelations sparked by these tales coax them to tell their own stories. So, what's the tea?

PRODUCTION HISTORY

Sweet Tea received its world premiere at About Face Theatre (Artistic Director, Bonnie Metzgar) in Chicago, Illinois, on April 29, 2010. The show was produced by Jane M. Saks and the Ellen Stone Belic Institute for the Study of Women and Gender in the Arts and Media, Columbia College, and About Face Theater. The production was directed by Daniel Alexander Jones. The scenic design was by Grant Sabin, lighting design by Kathy A. Perkins, sound design by Misha Fiksel and Miles Polaski, costume design by Janice Pytel, properties design by Joel William Lambie and dramaturgy by Chloe Johnston; the production stage manager was Donald Claxon. All roles were played by E. Patrick Johnson.

Sweet Tea—The Play went on to seven additional productions (as of this publication), all produced or coproduced by Jane M. Saks, with all roles played by E. Patrick Johnson.

On September 9, 2010, *Sweet Tea* was produced at the John L. Warfield Center (Artistic Director, Omi Osun Joni L. Jones) at the University of Texas in Austin, Texas. The production was directed by Helga Davis, with set design by Tramaine Berryhill, lighting consultant Kathy A. Perkins, sound design by Misha Fiksel and Miles Polaski, and costume design by Janice Pytel. The production stage manager was Natalie Goodnow.

On September 11, 2011, *Sweet Tea* debuted in Washington, D.C., at Signature Theatre (Artistic Director, Eric Schaeffer). The production was directed by Rajendra Ramoon Maharaj, with scenic design by Klyph Stanford, lighting design by Curtis V. Hodge, sound design by Matt Rowe, and costume design by Kathleen Geldard. The production stage manager was Nicole O. Leonard.

On February 13, 2014, *Sweet Tea* was produced at the Durham Arts Council in North Carolina. The production was directed by Joseph Megel, with scenic design by David Navalinski, lighting design by Kathy A. Perkins, sound design by Misha Fiksel, costume design by Marissa Erickson, choreography by Thomas DeFrantz, and projection design by Alex Maness. The ritual consultant was Renée Alexander Craft, and the production stage manager was Mary Forester.

On April 12, 2014, *Sweet Tea* was produced at Rites and Reasons Theatre (Artistic Director, Karen Baxter) in Providence, Rhode Island. The production was directed by Joseph Megel, with scenic design by David Navalinski, lighting design was by Kathy A. Perkins, sound design by Misha Fiksel, costume design by Marissa Erickson, choreography by Thomas DeFrantz, and projection design by Alex Maness. The ritual consultant was Renée Alexander Craft, and the production stage manager was Kathleen Moyer.

On April 29, 2015, *Sweet Tea* had its Los Angeles premiere at Towne Street Theater (Artistic Director, Nancy Cheryl Bellamy-Davis). The production was directed by Joseph Megel, with scenic design by David Navalinski, lighting design by Nathan Bellamy, sound design by Misha Fiksel, costume design by Marissa Erickson, choreography by Thomas DeFrantz, and projection design by Alex Maness. The ritual consultant was Renée Alexander Craft, and the production stage manager was Nathan Bellamy.

On May 28, 2015, *Sweet Tea* was produced at the Virginia Wadsworth Wirtz Performing Arts Center (Managing Director, Diane Claussen) in Evanston, Illinois. The production was coproduced by Jane M. Saks and Project&. It was directed by Joseph Megel, with scenic design by David Navalinski, lighting design by Nathan Bellamy, sound design by Misha Fiksel, costume design by Marissa Erickson, and choreography by Thomas DeFrantz. The projection design was by Alex Maness and

Nathan Lamp, the ritual consultant was Renée Alexander Craft, and the production stage manager was Amanda Landis.

On August 4, 2015, *Sweet Tea* premiered at the National Black Theatre Festival in Winston Salem, North Carolina. The production was co-produced by Jane M. Saks and Project&. It was directed by Joseph Megel, with scenic design was by David Navalinski and lighting design by Jim Davis based on the original lighting concept of Kathy A. Perkins. The sound design was by Misha Fiksel, costume design by Marissa Erickson, and choreography by Thomas DeFrantz. The projection design was by Alex Maness and Nathan Lamp, the ritual consultant was Renée Alexander Craft, and the production stage manager was Jameeka Holloway.

SWEET TEA

CHARACTERS

Countess Vivian. A ninety-three-year-old African American man from New Orleans; his accent is thick. He is spry and lucid despite his age and has a wicked sense of humor. He is dressed in aqua-blue polyester pants, a black and gray bowling shirt, and house slippers. He is a spiritual guide to EPJ.

EPJ. A thirty-eight-year-old African American male. He is a college professor, soft spoken and very approachable. He has a great singing voice. He is dressed in business casual clothes—slacks and button-down shirt and loafers.

Freddie. A sixty-two-year-old African American male. He is an effeminate, soft spoken, diminutive man with a very thick Georgia accent, who wears a scarf around his neck and multiple flashy rings on either hand. He is a professional painter who loves spinning stories.

Michael. A thirty-six-year-old African American male. He is immaculately dressed in a sports jacket and bow tie. He overenunciates his words, despite his heavy eastern North Carolina accent.

Duncan. A forty-five-year-old African American male. He is a commanding presence with a deep voice that fills the room. He speaks in a distinctive staccato rhythm. Born in Kansas City, Missouri, he has spent much of his life as an activist in Atlanta. He wears reading glasses on the tip of his nose and a minister's stole, and he carries a fan, which he uses with dramatic flair.

Gerome. A forty-seven-year old African American male. He is diminutive and speaks in a sing-song voice. He is conflicted about his sexuality and spirituality, which is reflected in his ideas about both topics. He is a religious zealot and a gay sympathizer all in one. He wears a preacher's robe with a very glitzy lining.

C. C. A forty-year-old African American male. He is a professor of dance and moves accordingly. He was born in Mississippi but divides his time between Alabama and New York City. He has a unique speaking voice that is raspy and slurry at the same time. He wears loungewear.

Stephen. A twenty-one-year-old African American male. He is a college theater major. He is dark-skinned, lanky, and has a very deep voice. He is very masculine. He wears a form-fitting tank top.

D. C. A fifty-three-year-old African American male. A retired schoolteacher, musician, and former football player, D.C. has a rugged exterior and lots of machismo. He is what one would describe as "hard." He wears a football jersey. While he is from Louisiana, he does not have a very noticeable accent.

R. Dioneaux. A forty-two-year-old African American male. R. Dioneaux is a former college professor. He has an edge to him that might make people uncomfortable. His voice is gravelly, and he speaks in rapid-fire fashion. He also has a verbal tic in which he pauses in mid-sentence to make what sounds like a growl. He wears a dashiki and multiple African bead necklaces.

Chaz/Chastity. A thirty-six-year-old African American gender-non-conforming person who mostly presents as female. Chaz is a hairdresser and has a soft, raspy voice with a slight western North Carolina accent. Chastity wears dramatic earrings and a feather boa.

Harold. A sixty-nine-year-old African American male. Harold is a "gentle giant" as he stands six feet, five inches, but has a sweet disposition. He is from St. Louis, Missouri, but has lived in the South long enough to have an accent. He wears big frame glasses and a cardigan.

*One actor may play all the characters, or they may be played by up to twelve different actors. If all the characters are played by one actor, the director must determine transitions. Costumes can be kept in the trunk for the actor to retrieve for this purpose. If there are multiple actors, the actor playing EPJ should remain onstage for most of the play, observing and listening to the other characters' stories, which prompt him to tell his own.

SETTING AND PROPS

The present. The set design can be as elaborate or as simple as the designer desires, but there should be a tea cart on wheels. On top of the cart there should be four water glasses, an ice bucket filled with ice, a mason jar filled with sugar (two cups), a mason jar filled with tap water, a long wooden spoon, a glass pitcher, and a mason jar filled with unsweetened tea. On the second shelf of the cart there should be a tea service box with twelve compartments. Eleven of the compartments should contain a votive filled with a different color sugar to represent each of the characters (not counting EPJ). The box can be camouflaged to look like a copy of the book *Sweet Tea: Black Gay Men of the South*. Also on stage should be a trunk from which props and costumes are taken, a Victorian-style chair, and a small side table. Somewhere upstage there should be an altar constructed from a small narrow table draped in mud cloth. Propped against the altar should be a walking stick.

Other props include a teapot (filled with freshly brewed tea); a black-and-white photograph of a nineteenth-century southern home; a sugar canister, an artist's paintbrush; an easel; a church fan; a handkerchief; an open-face tambourine; a wineglass; a half-drunk bottle of "wine"; a toothpick; a candle (with something to light it or, if fire code prohibits real fire, a battery-operated candle); a tin of old-fashioned candies; and a photograph of Countess Vivian (unless the actor playing Countess Vivian reappears onstage).

PROJECTIONS

The names of each character and their hometown can be projected onto a screen or scrim that is a part of the set design, such as a folding screen or some other flat surface. If the production has a projection designer, they could design an animated map of the South that calls up each character's hometown, followed by their name, when the character is introduced; otherwise, the name and hometown as called out in the script will suffice. The projection fades out when the character begins to speak. The projection designer might also create images to be projected for rituals.

EPJ's rituals can be improvised, but should include the items specified in the script.

[COUNTESS VIVIAN *is onstage five minutes before curtain, futzing about the tea cart. At curtain he goes offstage and returns with the teapot filled with warm, freshly brewed tea.*]

[Projection: "Countess Vivian—New Orleans"]

[COUNTESS VIVIAN *pours freshly brewed hot tea from the teapot into the glass pitcher; he will interrupt his tea-making from time to time to tell a story and then pick it back up as he remembers.*]

COUNTESS VIVIAN: They nickname me Vivian way, way, way, way long ago when I was young, young, young. Some of them older sissies give me that name, Vivian. And then down the line somebody put that other attachment to it, "The Countess."

[COUNTESS VIVIAN *picks up the mason jar on the cart and pours a long, steady stream of sugar into the pitcher of brewed tea until the mason jar is empty; he stirs the sugar and tea with the wooden spoon.*]

Of course, don't nobody call me that today 'cept folks who knew me way, way, way, way, way long ago when I was young, young, young, young, young. The young people today don't know nothing 'bout my nickname being Vivian. 'Course it really doesn't matter, 'cause people forget and they don't ask and you don't go telling.

[COUNTESS VIVIAN *clinks the spoon on the pitcher and puts it down on the cart.*]

I was born here in New Orleans on November the twelfth, 1912.

[COUNTESS VIVIAN *walks to the trunk, opens it, and pulls out a black-and-white photograph of a house.*]

We lived in a great big old house—two stories. We lived in what was called the Seventh Ward. In the beginning, when I was still like that [*miming his height*], we were on Marais Street. [*Pointing to the photograph*] It's further back this way [*pointing upstage*], where the project is today. It wasn't like it is today, I can tell you that.

[COUNTESS VIVIAN *places the photograph on top of the trunk and goes back to the cart to finish making tea.*]

Because everything was segregated. At that time, I did not know or realize that they had white sissies, 'cause they lived over on that side of the tracks.

[COUNTESS VIVIAN *pours water from the mason jar into the pitcher of tea and begins stirring.*]

And the only time you would come over here in the French Quarter would be if you was *working*. You could come over here and scrub the floor and clean the toilet and things like that, but you couldn't go hang in a bar and buy a drink or something like that. You couldn't do that. But you could have in your own areas on the other side of the tracks.

[COUNTESS VIVIAN *clinks the spoon on the side of the pitcher, puts it down on the cart, and walks downstage to the chair to tell another story.*]

We had sissies that used to wear dresses and hustle at night. They wouldn't have nothing in the room but the bed and the one chair. And that one chair would be like at that door right there [*pointing stage right*], and the bed maybe be way over that way somewhere [*pointing stage left*]. And you have somebody in that room right there [*pointing stage right*] and we used to call them "creeeeeeeep-ers" and they would get a trick, and they would [*miming the action of "creeping"*] creeeeeeeep in the door, creeeeeep to come in the door, and while the trick was busy doing his business, the creepers would go in his pocket and steal his money.

[COUNTESS VIVIAN *laughs at the memory and sits in the chair.*]

That went on for God knows how long, honey. That's why they didn't have nothing in the room, because if it gets to be too big a haul, then they have to get out of there, right? Because the people would go get the police. And then many, many, many, many times the person that got robbed wouldn't even go get the police because they would be ashamed to go and tell the police that they were up there with these black hookers, if they didn't know he was a sissy; they thought it was a woman. And even if it was a real woman they didn't want people to know that they was in there with these blacks. [*Seriously*] Because, you know, at that time blacks and whites wasn't close. Of course, they're not all that close now. But then, too, they were further apart than we are today. That is correct.

[COUNTESS VIVIAN *remembers the tea, returns to the cart, and begins filling glasses with ice and then with tea.*]

In '83 I developed cancer of the colon. And I had an operation. And then I had radiation therapy for about six or eight weeks. And I was told at that time that if I would live five years I would be doing alright. Well, I done lived. I done this since '83. So, I guess I'll keep on going.

[COUNTESS VIVIAN *pushes the cart downstage and begins passing out glasses of tea to audience members.*]

Don't let them set me in that chair, holding my hand, twiddling my thumbs because that's not gonna help at all. And set to worry about this or worry about that. You know, I just don't let things worry me. And I don't have too many aches. Just sometimes I get stiff and things like that. But after I start walking or moving all about it's all gone.

[COUNTESS VIVIAN *pushes the cart back to its original position.*]

And the only medications I take now is a few aspirins sometimes. And I keep my Alka-Seltzer. And to keep my beauty up, I uses Oil of Olay. That's right, child. I hope to tell you. Because I know people that's way, way, way, way, way younger than me who look woooorse than me. So, I say I'm blessed. That's right, honey. 'Cause I done outlived all of my family and I'm going to be here until after a lot of them other one's gone, too. I hope to tell you.

'Cause the young people today, don't know what we been through, honey. They just go, go, go, go, go, but it seem to me, in order to know where you going, you gotta know where you come from. That is correct. Evvvverybody got to go through and *live* to *know*. The Bible say, "Seek and ye shall find," but you ain't going to find nothing if you don't know what you're looking for, honey. I hope to tell you. [*Walking over to the trunk and picking up the photograph*] I remember years ago, this young man come here say he writing a book on the gays; he want me to tell my story. [*Lifting the lid of the trunk*] I looked at him and I think to myself, he don't want me to tell *my* story, [*placing the photograph inside the trunk*] he need to tell his *own*. [*Closing the lid of the trunk*] Everybody got a story to tell.

[COUNTESS VIVIAN *taps the top of the trunk, winks, and then exits.*]

EPJ [*singing from offstage*]:

Hush, hush, somebody's calling my name
Hush, hush, somebody's calling my name
Hush, hush, somebody's calling my name
Oh, my Lord, Oh, my Lord, what shall I do? What shall I do?

[Projection: "Elondust Patrick Johnson—Hickory, North Carolina"]

[EPJ *enters and directly addresses the audience.*]

EPJ: My name is Elondust Patrick Johnson. Since no one can pronounce my first name, I go by E. Patrick. I'm the baby of my family—the seventh child of Miss Sarah. I was born in Hickory, North Carolina, population thirty-five thousand (on a good day) and known as "the furniture capital of the world." Like many small southern towns, Hickory still has a set of railroad tracks that separates the north side of town and the south side of town—whites to the north and blacks to the south. The city is patterned after Washington, D.C., and divided into four directional quadrants—northeast, northwest, southeast, southwest. I grew up at two-twenty-nine Eighth Avenue Drive, Southwest, in the Ridgeview community where most of the blacks lived. And although *Brown vs. Board of Education* became law in 1954, schools in Hickory were not fully integrated until 1973, the year I entered first grade. I am the first African American born in Hickory to earn a Ph.D. So, on July 20, 1996, my hometown celebrates "Dr. E. Patrick Johnson Day." The ceremony is held in the old black high school gymnasium, Ridgeview High School. [*Walking over to the altar and picking up the walking stick*] Instead of a key to the city, I receive a hickory stick! [*Holding up the stick*] The two running themes of my day are "They Said It Couldn't Be Done" and "From a Zero to a Hero." While I never considered myself a "zero," I understood that the black folks of Ridgeview were thumbing their noses at them, the white folks on the north side of the railroad tracks who said it couldn't be done. But what the Ridgeview community doesn't know is that it wasn't just my being black, but also me being gay, that motivated my overachievement. It was the sense that, if I could focus attention away from some of the fundamental parts of who I was coming to know as "me"—by working extra hard for the "A" in school, by joining every possible high school club and becoming senior class president, by working my soprano voice to out-sing all of

EPJ (E. Patrick Johnson) laments not coming out to his community.

the girls in the soprano section in the church choir, by agreeing to give speeches and lectures for the community to inspire young kids to stay in school and off drugs, and by being the "good" son who sends money home to help out—then and only then, perhaps, when the news finally came that I am gay, it wouldn't be so damn disappointing.

I stood before my hometown, as I stand before you now, and tell them the story that they want to hear, but not the one that I *must* tell, which is the truth—my truth. But to get there, I had to bear witness.

[EPJ *kneels in front of the trunk, resting the walking stick on the floor. He lifts the top of the trunk and withdraws a clear glass canister half full of sugar, which has a lid and attached scooper, and places it on top of the trunk. He then walks over to the tea cart, and during the following speech, he picks up the tea service from the bottom shelf of the cart, holds it between his two hands—one on the bottom and one on the top—and slowly walks back to the trunk.*]

And so, I went on a journey back to the South in search of answers and started listening to my brothers' stories, fathers' stories, sons' stories, granddaddies' stories, great granddaddies' stories, so that I could tell my own.

[EPJ *kneels behind the trunk and places the tea service on the trunk lid; he twists the lid off the container of sugar and then opens the tea service, which prompts the sound of a drone in a minor key over which there are the sounds of rattles and a shekere. EPJ chants, similar to a black folk sermon, while methodically and ritualistically pouring the different colors of sugar from the votives in the tea service into the glass container of sugar, replacing each votive in the tea service after it is emptied.*]

EPJ (E. Patrick Johnson) begins the sugar ritual.

I need to walk the path to truth paved by my queer ancestors both living and dead. I need to hear their tales and touch their scars before I can go home as who I am. Hush! Hush! They are calling me to story. There is power in the story. Hush! Hush! They are calling me to story. The beauty of truth and the beauty of story are ready to meet.

[EPJ *closes the tea service lid on the word "meet." The sound effects end. He methodically screws the lid back on the glass container of mixed sugars.*]

If you want the truth, [*placing the walking stick on top of the trunk*] you start the truth at the beginning.

[EPJ *stands and walks to the tea cart.*]

In the beginning was the word. [*Picking up the mason jar of tea from the cart*] And the word was [*Holding up the jar as if offering it to a god*] the tea.

[*Blackout;* EPJ *places the tea on the side table and walks over to the trunk to get the tea service and sugar container.*]

[Projection: "Freddie—Madison, Georgia"]

[FREDDIE *enters singing "Georgia on my Mind" and carrying a paintbrush and an easel.* EPJ *watches* FREDDIE *while placing the tea service and sugar container on the altar—the container on top of the tea service. He props the walking stick on the side of the altar and then perches upstage and listens to* FREDDIE.]

Georgia, Georgia,
The whole day through
An' just an old sweet song
Keeps Georgia on my mind.

FREDDIE [*mimes painting*]: I was born in Madison, Georgia, on May twelfth, 1944. My childhood was awful. Oh, God, it was awful.

[FREDDIE *abruptly stops mime painting and sits in the chair to tell the story.*]

I was an unwanted child—an *unexpected* child and an unwanted child. I'm the fifth child but, after four children, I think the doctors told my mother she couldn't conceive any more children. And then I came along, so I was sort of a surprise in that regard. But my father's mother was a very strong figure in my father's life, and . . . You saw the movie *Roots*? You know how they held the baby up? I kind of use that analogy.

[FREDDIE *gets up from his chair and mimes the "Kunta Kinte" moment from* Roots.]

My grandmother held me up and declared that none of her blood was in me, which meant that her son was not my father. So my father, being the weakling that he was, believed her. So that caused my grandmother and my father to treat me differently.

[FREDDIE *goes back to the easel and mimes painting.*]

One of the more painful examples I can remember is my sister and I being on the school grounds of Bernie Street Elementary School—it's no longer there but it was the colored school in Madison, Georgia—and us running out to the edge of the schoolyard to my father and asking him for a nickel. And he pulled out a handful of change and would give my sister a nickel and wouldn't give me one, saying he didn't have anymore. And I remember crying and that kind of thing. And I think the most painful memory I have is that of my father's cousin, A.C. I don't know how that was spelled, but we called him Cousin A.C. His wife's name was Maja. And their last name is Talbert. Cousin Maja said to my mother one day (my mother was named Annie Belle, but everybody called her Bea). She said, "Bea, why don't you give Freddie to me since Aunt Evvie . . ." (whose name was Eva, but who they called Evvie) "and W.S. . . ." (my father . . . my father's name is Washington Smithson Styles but he was simply known as W.S., his initials); anyway, she said, "Why don't you give Freddie to me since Aunt Evvie and W.S. don't want him?" with me standing there.

[FREDDIE *puts the paintbrush down on the easel and moves downstage.*]

[*Somberly*] And I remember starting to cry and hugging my mother around the legs. And I must have been very young because my mother was only five feet, two inches, and I remember my head was about at her knee. So, I was a very small child. And I remember crying and saying, "Mama, you gonna to give me away?" and she said, "No." [*Beat.*] Those are the more painful memories I have of early childhood in Madison, Georgia. [*Returns to painting*] And I've been in counseling and cried through all of this stuff. I don't know if you know this or not, but counseling is a scary process. You have to really be able to, I think, open those doors. And you also have to be able to, I think, admit or to give up on what I call a prevalent myth in the black community, this sainted mother myth. You have to see her for who she is. That just because she's your mother, she's [*punctuating each word with a stroke*] not a saint.

[FREDDIE *stops painting and takes a seat, still holding the brush.*]

The abuse I suffered at the hands of my mother was certainly abuse, but early on I kind of understood that it was about her. That she was tormented. You see, it didn't matter how badly she abused us, her saving grace was always, "At least I didn't give you away." Because my mother was given away as an infant. The story I've heard is that my grandmother was very young when my mother was born and her father gave my mother to some other people when my grandmother wasn't at home one day. And so my mother never forgave her mother for giving her away. But she was very angry and tormented and very abusive of my sister and I. And her saving grace was always, "At least I didn't give you away." So, early on, I realized that my mother had a problem and I couldn't depend on her to protect me. But along the way I was kind of protected by other people.

In high school, even in elementary school, there was one teacher in particular who would assign a girl to tell her if anybody bothered me when she went out of the room. I later found out that she was, in fact, a lesbian. And was a *married* lesbian. She had a husband and some children, but she was, in fact, a lesbian. And she would assign a girl to tell her. In high school, there was always a bigger boy or somebody who would kind of protect me. And the bigger boys, I never had sex with them but they just kind of had a sense that I needed protecting.

[FREDDIE *gets out of the chair.*]

When I was in sixth grade, some boys were bothering me and the teacher kept us after school. And I would carry a single-edge razor blade [*looking at the paintbrush as if it's the razor*] in my pocket to sharpen my pencils. The boys were going to line up to beat me up because they said it was my fault that we were kept after school. So, I would always say in the sweetest little voice, because you see I'm reasonably soft spoken now: "Leave me alone. I'm minding my business. Don't bother me." So, this boy ran up to hit me and I [*miming the cutting with his paintbrush*] cut him across his shoulder with the razor blade. And by that time, the teacher came and said, "You boys better go home." So, the last thing I heard him say was, "You're a mean sissy. I'm going to have your ass locked up."

The next day I went to school. And this same boy came up to me and he had a hairline cut on his shoulder because I had cut through two or three layers of clothing. And he said, "You better be glad." I said, "Listen, do not bother . . . I keep telling you to leave me alone. I want to be left alone. I'm not bothering you. Don't bother me."

[FREDDIE *returns to painting.*]

And what always happened if anybody attacked me, they always ended up seeing some of their blood. So, rumors spread. "Don't bother him. He's a mean little sissy and he's stronger than he looks."

[FREDDIE *exits with the easel and paintbrush.*]

[Projection: "EPJ"]

EPJ [*watching Freddie exit and then rushing to speak*]: I wasn't a "mean little sissy." I was a *nice fat* sissy. I wore a size called "husky." Can you imagine going shopping with your mother and hearing the clerk say, "Oh, I think he's going to need a husky"? Add to that my big butt, high voice, and lisp, and you have the making of the homophobic bully's wet dream. I didn't get picked on as much as some others whose flame burned a bit brighter than mine, but, like Freddie, I could fight if pushed to the edge. And Scotty Davidson had it coming.

[EPJ *solicits audience participation to repeat the line, "Scotty had it coming" when directed.*]

[*Pointing to the audience*] Scotty had it coming. Scotty Davidson was the only one-hundred-percent white boy living in the projects. Everybody else was either one-hundred-percent black or fifty-percent black (especially his two little sisters). [*Pointing to the audience*] Scotty had it coming. I'm making my mud pies and he's making his mud pies and my mud pies are minding their own business until Scotty makes it his business to knock over my mud pies. "Faggot mud pies." [*Pointing to the audience*] Scotty had it coming. I'm catching my bees and he's catching his bees. And my bees are minding their own business until Scotty makes it his business to let my bees go. "You caught sissy bees." [*Pointing to the audience*] Scotty had it coming. [*In schoolgirl voice*] My butt is big and my butt is high and my butt is minding its own business, until Scotty makes it his business to try and kick my butt. "You got a girl butt." But, when they finally pull me off of him, I pull a Mike Tyson and take a little bit of his ear with me. [*Pointing to the audience*] Scotty had it coming. Wherever he is today, Scotty Davidson is still a white boy, but he's no longer one hundred percent.

[EPJ *snaps his fingers; blackout on snap.* EPJ *returns to his perch upstage.*]

[MICHAEL *enters, preening in an imaginary mirror.*]

[Projection: "Michael—Raleigh, North Carolina"]

MICHAEL: I have always been very proper. Had a flair and a knack for grammar and presentation. And a look that I think most African Americans at that particular time did not have. You know, I didn't cut grass and do the traditional things that most boys my age would do. I shopped, you know, I shopped and that was my interest. But I played sports. I ran track, I played baseball, I did eight years of gymnastics, and I tried football and I dislocated my shoulder playing football and that ended that. I just always knew I was not the most masculine man.

[MICHAEL *moves to the chair and sits.*]

Michael (E. Patrick Johnson) preens in his suit
while discussing being "proper."

But in terms of my sexuality, I don't think individuals are necessarily born gay, because I chose to date men. And so that's a choice I made. And to me, it's just sex. But if I fell in love with a woman, it wouldn't bother me if I never slept with a man again, because it would not change my personality.

So, everybody in my family knows, you know, in my immediate family, in particular, and then of course, all my aunts and uncles know, my grandmothers know. It was not easy for me. [*Getting up from the chair*] For example, when I had this twenty-first birthday party, my father was the first person to ever say, he pulled me to the side and he told me happy birthday, he gave me money and whatever. He said, "Someone said X is gay," you know, this guy I was talking to. And I said, "Really?" And he said, "People will say cruel things." And that was it. And I had friends who would call the house or whatever and my brother, who was in high school or junior high at that time, would say, "Michael, some fag is on the phone for you." And I would say, "Give me the phone, boy," and whatever.

My mother's sorors would call, you know. I'd see them at the mall. And before I could get home, my mother would say, "Well, Michael, such-and-such called and said you were at the mall with some gay boys or running around with some gay boys." And, you know, I would laugh and just go on or whatever. But I think the straw that broke the camel's back was when I was modeling for a major boutique-ish type of store here, and moved from that to one of my cousin's stores where she does hair. And I had this high-top fade thing. And she asked me to do this hair show for her. And I said yeah. She said, "Well, you going to let me perm your hair?" And I said, "Girl, whatever you want to do, long as you're going to pay me." Well, she permed it. And after it permed, it fell down here [*pointing to his brow*]. And it was this really pretty long bang. And she said, "That's so pretty." And, you know, because this [*using both hands to point to either side of his head*] was cut off and I had this big slope thing. And when it fell, it was just here, so she just cut and curled this bang. And I went home to my parents. And my father was doing the hedges. And I got out and I'm walking, you know. And I just never pay any attention to my father, I really don't. And I'm going up the steps and he grabs my bang and he tries to cut my hair with these hedge clippers. And I'm hollering like a girl, "Daddy, Daddy, you know, what you doing? You're messing up my hair." And so, my mother comes out and she says, you know, "Leave him alone," and, you know. And it ended. And, of course, you know me. I go right back to the salon and get my hair done again. So, I never paid any attention to what people said, you know. I just always felt confident about myself and the gay issue never bothered me. But you better not say anything to me about it, you know. People have always been afraid to approach me about whether I'm gay or not. They may think whatever—but they're not going to say anything.

[MICHAEL *exits.*]

[Projection: "EPJ"]

[EPJ *enters.*]

EPJ: I didn't have a "bang," but I did have mama's wigs. Mama first dressed me in a wig at the age of three. She thought it was so cute. But then I started putting the wigs on myself. There was something about the feel of all that curly hair on top of my head that freed me. Before long, I was experimenting with Mama's lipstick, necklaces, and high heels. Her room became a playhouse for me to experiment. Mama had cute drag and I loved being up in it.

[EPJ *sings "When Sunday Comes" (after singer Daryl Coley) and sits upstage right.*]

When Sunday
When Sunday
When Sunday comes

[Projection: "Duncan—Atlanta, Georgia"]

[DUNCAN *enters, sashaying across the stage and scanning the audience over his reading glasses. He is holding his fan.*]

DUNCAN: Honey, church didn't *play* in my upbringing. It *was* my upbringing. When your father is the pastor and the church is less than two hundred people, that is your extended family. I enjoyed going to church because I was a leader at church. And church was, at times, just a little bit safer. And especially after my voice changed and I became quite a good baritone singer at church. So not only was I gifted and rewarded for my intelligence and my abilities at church, but I was loved and admired and I got all the stuff that they claim we don't get as young black kids. But I got it.

[DUNCAN *sits on top of the trunk.*]

When it came to gay folks, I'm very careful about this one because I don't buy the mythology that black folks are more homophobic than anybody else. And the reason I don't buy it is because I grew up knowing gay people, and they were all in the church. And I'm not talking gay, I'm talking flaming queens who ran the choirs.

[DUNCAN *gets up and paces.*]

I met James Cleveland as a child. And the Troubadours, who were an all-male group, and none of them were butch. And I met the Hawkins Family. Yes, I'm gonna say it. [*Beat.*] I met Edwin and Walter Hawkins and their entourage and their family before they were out, some of them. I won't out all of them. But I will say those that are out now, I met them before they were out. And so, there was this silence around their sexual orientation, but they were present.

And we're in church because everything is full of gay men. Because that's our calling—to be spiritual leaders. Not abominations, but the folk running the thing. Because in every denomination, if you look around and you look close enough, you'll say, [*fanning dramatically*] "Oh my!" And it's not just Christians. I mean, the Indians and Hindus have the sect of transgender folk who roam from city to city. You can't get rid of us. You can't even have your faith without us. I mean, of course the black church presence in the community *is* because it's ours. It's our institution. If you're going to have an institution in the black community, you need educated, sensitive, articulate, bright young men running it. [*Beat.*] And guess who that just described?

[DUNCAN *fans dramatically while looking over the top of his glasses.*]

Duncan (E. Patrick Johnson) challenges the notion
that the church shuns gays.

You know, James Baldwin said that we couldn't enter the twenty-first century without him, and he was so right because they're teaching his words in English classes. A black gay man who came out of church.

[DUNCAN *exits.*]

[EPJ *stands and sings "His Eye is on the Sparrow."*]

> *I sing because I'm happy*
> *I sing because I'm free*
> *His eye is on the sparrow,*
> *and I know he watches me*

[*On the last word of the song,* GEROME *enters, his voice booming over* EPJ*'s, singing.*]

[Projection: "Gerome—Tuscaloosa, Alabama"]

GEROME [*singing, drawing out each "yes"*]: Somebody say yes, yes, yes.

[GEROME *looks very seriously at the audience before speaking, his arms stretched wide, his body turning from side to side.*]

[*Free associating*] I think that homosexuality is a . . . I'm coming with it now. I think that it's wrong, as far as right and wrong. I think that God loves the homosexual—the person—but He hates what they do. I don't think that He condones a man [*beat*] being with a man. And for me to not be able to just turn it off like I would like to if I could. I don't want no wife. I know that. I don't want no parts of no female as a sex partner. [*Almost as an aside*] Other than my friend or my sister, you know, something like that, or a teacher as a female friend. [*Back to audience*] I believe in the Bible and I believe that He said somewhere in there that He would "rather you be as you are, but if you cannot contain yourself . . ."—I think He's talking about sexually—"it is better to marry than not." [*As an aside*] So, I think that I would like to live my life single, you know, free of any sexual conduct, none of that.

[*To audience, harshly*] I believe that He will move it [*beat*] if you're *serious*. If you really want it gone. 'Cause see, some of us go to God playing, you know. Like, "I really want to let go, Lord." Then He'll get you out of it and then you end up backsliding. You ever heard of the word "backsliding?" Okay. [*To himself*] That's what happened to me one time, you know and I was too young and stupid to know what I was doing. But, after I've gone through, gone through, gone through, I do believe that it will be a thing of the past. [*To audience*] Oooh, if you only knew where I come *from*, you know. I left it up to Him to deliver me out of this. I mean, ask yourself. Do you believe that it's pleasing to God? I mean, any person with a drop of God in him would know it's unnatural, it's not right. I don't think we was put here to just wallow with each other and party to party. You know, people go too far. I mean just think, say, [*pointing at audience members*] if you've got two or three friends and their two or three friends got a friend and a friend, and they're just criss-crossing and all this, some sickness, something's gonna kick off in their wrong. He will reveal to you. [*To himself*] No matter how lustful I may feel or whatever, "Fight the urge, Gerome."

[*To audience*] Okay. Let me see if I can break this down to you very clear. Right now, I'm a bit disappointed in the churches. Not God. Not the buildings. But people. They have just smeared [*pulling a handkerchief from his robe and wiping his brow*] how can I put this [*beat*] feces [*making a smearing motion with the handkerchief*] all over it. It's sad what preachers are doing now, getting in the pulpits and gay bashing. "God created Adam and Eve, not Adam and Steve." That's tacky. For a person to say that God called him, when God is so intelligent and so wise until He don't even ordain a person that hadn't grown past that level. To stand there

Gerome (E. Patrick Johnson) preaches a conflicted sermon
about homosexuality.

and stab at some of His children that are wrestling with what gay
people wrestle with. They are driving away the ones that I think
God really called. [*More agitated*] Because He said He came for the
sinners. He didn't come for the perfect, the uprighteous. He came
for the [*pointing at a different person for each word*] lesbians! Ho-
mosexuals! Murderers! Thieves! Backbiters! Liars! These are the
ones that the Church, this building, is for. So, I look at it now as a
whole picture, to say that society and hypocritical hypocrites have
picked out gays to point at. And it's a nasty thing what they're doing. The Holy Spirit lets me know every day when I get up, [*grabs
the tambourine from the side table, sermonizing*] "Gerome, I'm
with you. I love you." Something speaks to my heart, letting me
know, "Get up and do another day. It looks cloudy today. It's go-

ing to be a little dreary, but go on regardless to what the [*shaking the tambourine*] old sissies are saying about you. Go on, regardless to what the [*shaking the tambourine*] young sissies are saying about you. Go on, Gerome, regardless to what the [*hopping on both legs*] church hoppers are saying about you. Go on, regardless to what relatives, neighbors, friends are saying about you. [*Full out preaching*] Don't look left. Don't look right. Just go on. Keep your eyes on Me. Know how you treat your coworkers. Know how you treat your neighbors. Know how to treat these people. [*Ecstatic*] Be kind! Be kind! Be kind! And I'll bless you!"

[*Gospel shouting music starts up and* GEROME *begins a "holy dance" around the stage and maybe into the audience; when the music stops, he turns to the audience and delivers the next line.*]

Now, don't you think it's time for this one to end? 'Cause I done gone too far.

[*The music starts again and* GEROME *"shouts" until he's offstage.*]

[*Lights dim, but not to full blackout.* EPJ *sings "More Like Jesus." from offstage.*]

To be like Jesus
To be like Jesus
Oh I how I long to be like Him
Meek and lowly, humble and holy
Oh how I long to be like Him

[Projection: "C.C.—Greenwood, Mississippi"]

[C.C. *enters with* GEROME's *tambourine and puts it on the side table. He then opens the trunk and pulls out a glass and a bottle of red wine and sits on the floor by the trunk.*]

c.c. [*pouring a glass of wine*]: My father really couldn't stand people who was in churches, 'cause he thought they were all ignorant. For him it was like all these people who was irresponsible and, "Oh, the Lord's going to take care of the garden." He really had issues with that. And so later him and I would have these incredible conversations about God. "Can you believe the shit they saying up in these churches?" So, I've been exposed to all kinds of faiths. I think I've been Catholic. Methodist. I've been sprinkled. I've been sanctified. I joined all of it, baby. Dunked underwater, over the water, walked on water. So, those years were very formative for me and still remain.

[c.c. *takes a sip of wine.*]

The church was like a safe haven, especially for gay people. People still try to deny it, but the church is full of gay people. There are more gay people in church than at the bars. So even as a young child, you begin to like put two and two together. But when I got old enough to understand what was being said, then yeah, I had to like let it go 'cause I never understood what I called those "church sissies." And what I mean by that is they're everywhere. And Atlanta and all is full of 'em. And mind you, I thank God they're there and so I don't want to say anything bad about them, but I never understood that concept of people going places where you were going to be *bashed*. How could you find Jesus up in there? So I, on purpose, avoided what I called "church sissies." Like all those church sissies, I stayed away from them because that was a little too crazy for me. Flippin' over all those benches and all that stuff and then, at the end of the night, you're gonna be like in bed with somebody in the name of hate? 'Cause you have to hate yourself. So, I ain't never want none of that bad hate sex at all, so I stayed away from churches. [*Sipping wine*] Mine is really church without walls. I walk around this house every day and talk to God. Every-

C.C. (E. Patrick Johnson) discusses "church sissies"
and why he left the church.

thing I do is church. Thank God, I found peace with it. You just have to know Jesus for yourself and leave it at that.

The thing that I keep trying to tell you is most people never forgive themselves for being gay. [*Beat.*] It's just that simple. [*Beat.*] And that's why it has been the hardest thing, for me, to ever really truly deal with a black man. They neeeeeeeeever forgive themselves for being gay. [*Beat.*] And I think that no matter how painful or no matter how they could be bashed up in there, they still just feel like, "If I'm *there*, Jesus may not *really* see my other side, because I still think I'm a bad person." So, that's what that is.

[C.C. *exits and passes* EPJ, *who walks to the trunk and picks up the glass and wine bottle and places them in the trunk while speaking to the audience.*]

[Projection: "EPJ"]

EPJ: I was not one of those self-hating "church sissies" and my church wasn't homophobic. I attended "Morning Start First Baptist Church. The church where everybody is somebody and Jesus is Lord." Baby I believe it.

[EPJ *hops on top of the trunk.*]

Reverend Webster E. Lytle is our pastor and he is a sho 'nuff civil rights leader; he has us reciting Jesse Jackson's "I am somebody. [*Encouraging the audience to repeat after him:*] You are somebody. We are somebody" in Vacation Bible School. [*Pumping his fist*] Fists in the air. Our ushering uniforms are homemade animal-print dashikis.

[EPJ *jumps off the trunk.*]

I join the church and the children's choir at age six. My first solo is, "Somebody's Knocking at Your Door." Shut up! By the time I am twelve, I have made quite a reputation for myself as "the little fat boy with the high butt and high voice that can sing." I am the only boy in the soprano section and I can out-sing all of the girls. I get the church to shoutin' every Sunday by singing the solo originally sung by Yolanda Adams with the Southeastern Inspiration Choir out of Houston, Texas.

[*"My Liberty" begins to play and* EPJ *sings along for a few bars.*]

[*Caught in the reverie and reenacting the scene:*] I catch the spirit, and twirl down the aisle—all the while holding a note and daring anybody to take that microphone out of my hand. The little queen in me is begging to show out and I have a captive audience. Baby, it ain't the army where you can be all that you can be, it's the black church—that is, unless you belong to New Birth Missionary Baptist Church and Bishop Eddie Long is your pastor.

While visiting Atlanta in 1995, some friends took me to one of the services at New Birth, before it became a megachurch. Bishop Long's sermon on this special Saturday evening service was "Paying for the Sins of Your Father." He came into the pulpit with chains draped over his shoulders to represent the chains of sin that are binding us—sins that were not atoned for by our ancestors.

[EPJ *steps up on the trunk and declaims in a voice full of fire and brimstone:*]

"If you're a smoker, that means somebody in your family back in the day was a smoker and didn't take care of that, didn't ask God to take that craving away. If you fat—come on now! I'm going somewhere, I'm going somewhere. That means somebody in your family back in the day was fat and didn't take care of that. Sugar! High blood pressure. Gout! You wouldn't be dealing with any of these ailments if your ancestors had stayed prayed up. How many of you are praying with me this evening? Now, I'm getting ready to step on some toes. [*Making an evil face*] If you a faggot, that means somebody in your family back in the day was a faaaaaaag-gooooooot and didn't pray that sickness away."

[EPJ *steps down from the trunk and rolls his eyes.*]

The queens in the church, including some of my friends, went wild, running around the church dancing to their own damnation. [*Sitting on the trunk*] Well, I say karma is a bitch. For the Bishop settled a suit for twenty-five million dollars for having sexual relations with four young men. [*Beat.*] I guess somebody [*coyly*] in his family [*beat*] back in the day, didn't take care of it.

[*Old school house music begins to play lowly in the background, preferably the remix of Shirley Ceasar's "Hold My Mule." EPJ takes off his shirt to reveal a snug-fitting A-frame tank top; he drapes the button-up shirt over the back of the chair.*]

That night after church, my friends take me out dancing to a club called Tracks. We dance until the wee hours of the morning and when five A.M. rolls around, the mood of the club shifts and there is a feeling of anticipation in the air. The music shifts to what sounds like the "shout" music played in my church back home.

I look up and it's DJ Sedrick, the legendary House Mother of D.C., there to give us life on the dance floor. DJ Sedrick begins to do a roll call: "We got any L.A. in the house? Show your hands if you're from the gay mecca of D.C.! New York City? Chicago! And last, but not least, let me see the children from Hotlanta!" Then, he begins to testify:

[*Preacherly voice*] "Look around you. Somebody that was here last year ain't here tonight! Look around you! Somebody's brother, somebody's sister, somebody's cousin, somebody's uncle done gone on to the Maker. But Grace woke you up this morning! How many of you know what I'm talking about? If He's been good to you, let me see you wave your hands."

[EPJ *grabs the tambourine from the table.*]

A drag queen appears from nowhere and begins to walk around the side of the dance floor beating a tambourine to the beat of the rhythm. DJ Sedrick's preaching and the music works us into a frenzy. Pump it up, pump it up! Pump it up, pump it up!

[*The music swells and* EPJ *does a '90s dance routine and exits.*]

[STEPHEN *enters singing "Sometimes I Feel Like a Motherless Child" in a somber tone. During the last line of the song, he sits on the floor center stage, his knees pulled to his chest with his arms wrapped around them.*]

Sometimes I feel like a motherless child
Sometimes I feel like a motherless child
Sometimes I feel like a motherless child
A long way from home

[Projection: "Stephen—Tuscaloosa, Alabama"]

STEPHEN [*to himself*]: I was just wired differently, just was wired differently. And, I felt that I was being punished for being this way. And so from every angle, I was being told, "You've got it wrong." [*To audience*] I vividly remember my mom saying, "Don't you grow up to be no faggot." I *vividly* remember hearing that. I was really, really effeminate, and would get beat up a lot because of that. You're getting beat up at school 'cause you're a faggot, you're a little girl, you're a little sissy. And my mom was like, "Everybody is telling you this is wrong." And I struggled and I really wanted to kill myself. I wanted to die rather than continue to displease the God that I loved so much. Since I can't stop these feelings that I've been told are wrong, I would really prefer to die and be able to say I'm going to heaven than continue to live this way and go to hell because of this. [*Beat.*] And, it got to the point to where I made the realization that I believe in the God who is all-knowing. I believe in a God that doesn't make mistakes. I believe in a God that has created me. I believe that I'm not a mistake. I believe that this is the way that I was created. [*Beat.*] I didn't choose it. [*Beat.*] Who would choose it? [*Beat.*] It used to frustrate me so much being in the closet early on, and hear people say, "It's a choice. It's a lifestyle change." [*Angrily*] It's like you really don't understand my struggle. I've tried that. I've tried that. I read up on ex-gay therapies. I have tried to be what you thought Stephen should be, and I'm exhausted. [*Beat.*] I was headed for destruction. I was gonna have to come to terms with this 'cause it was something that I was ignoring for a long time, ignoring this fight within myself, that was killing me. And, it got to the point to where it was like, "No. No. From now on, what I believe is gonna be something that I find to be true for me and who Stephen is, not something that I've been fed since I was smaller."

[*Beat.*]

It is so easy to be loved for something that you're not, rather than to be hated for something that you are. You know what I mean? It's so easy.

[*Beat.*]

I guess the first time when I honestly stopped to think about it I was about seventeen years old and had a girlfriend. I really wasn't interested in a physical anything with her. I really wasn't. Sex was always an issue until finally, I thought, "Well, for me to prove myself as a man, we need to have sex." And, it was the first time I had sex. I fathered my son. And, it's like, although he is something that motivates me, someone, when I get exhausted, or when I really start to be like, "What am I working towards," he motivates me past those moments. But, it's one of the earliest moments where I was like, "You came to this point being something that you're not."

[*Beat.*]

Right before I got my first professional job doing theater in college, I had to leave for the summer. So, the day before I had to leave, I spent all day with my four-year-old son, Ledarius, and I explained to him who I was. [*Rising to one knee and speaking to his son:*] "The same way that your mom loves her husband, I feel the same way about other men. I don't know if you understand this or not.

More than likely, you'll probably be angry because you don't completely understand it, but come to me with that anger. Let's talk about it."

[*Long pause.* STEPHEN *rises to his feet.*]

It was surreal. It was like, [*beat*] here I am [*beat*] coming out to my son, the only person in my family that I've truly [*beat*] truly [*beat*] come out to.

[*After a beat,* STEPHEN *reprises the last line of the song.*]

A long way from home

[*As* STEPHEN *sings the last word and exits,* EPJ *enters.*]

[Projection: "EPJ"]

EPJ [*hesitantly*]: "Mom, I need to talk to you about something. There's something that I've wanted to talk to you about for some time now, but I haven't had the courage to say it."

[*In his mother's voice*] "What have you done?"

"I haven't done anything. I'm gay."

[*In his mother's voice*] "Pat, you mean to tell me that you like other men?"

"Yes, ma'am."

[*In his mother's voice, melodramatically*] "Why?"

"Mom, let me ask you something. Have you ever found yourself attracted to another woman?"

[*In his mother's voice, as if thinking aloud*] "No."

[*As if delivering a punchline*] "Neither have I."

[*In his mother's voice, resolutely*] "Well, if that's the way you are, I just have to accept it. You're my son and I love you."

But that acceptance doesn't come for some years later. She shares what I tell her with no one—not even her closest friends. When I move to Chicago with my partner, she says, "Pat, you're not going to buy a house with that *boy*, are you?" I do buy a house with that boy and after several more years pass, it finally clicks that this is not a phase. Our commitment ceremony is the crowning moment of the ten-year period in which my mother wrestles with my being gay, especially when she walks in with me at our ceremony and sees all of these straight people affirming our love. I tell people all the time that we come out to different people in different ways about many things all of our lives.

[*Beat.* EPJ *puts his hand on his hip and begins swaying from side to side.*]

I remember my mother carrying me on her hip, my body rocking back and forth with her sway. The sway that lulls church babies into gospel comas. When she stood, left arm akimbo, I learned that stance so that I could be close to the hip that mothered me into queerness, into my fabulousness. I knew then. I think my mother did too. Thirty something years later, she stands with me at a ceremony she doesn't quite understand and didn't want to attend, confronting the knowledge her hip instilled in me. In that moment, my mother came out, and gave herself permission to love her baby boy—all of him.

[*Fade to black and* EPJ *returns to his perch upstage right as* D.C. *enters, wearing a football jersey and chewing on a toothpick; he kicks the trunk as he passes it on his way over to the chair.*]

[Projection: "D.C.—Baton Rouge, Louisiana"]

D.C. [*moving the side table to in front of the chair and propping his feet up on it*]: At age fifty-three, I just fell in love with a guy. Everything else has been just [*claps his hands*] "wham bam, thank you ma'am." And this love thing, bug, hit me in mid-November, well about Christmas. [*Beat.*] The bug's dead. I had heard people say how it feels to have your heart broken. And I didn't know until then. It was like an elephant standing on my chest. I left town for a few days, and then I came back. It still wasn't right. I left for five more. I'm all right now because I have control of it. And because of that, *I*, that's a personal pronoun, I will not allow myself to fall in love with another guy again in my life.

[D.C. *takes his feet off the table and leans forward.*]

I have three guys right now. They all are my significant other. And I pretty much play them like roulette. Whichever one I feel today, whatever. However, they don't have that same calendar.

[D.C. *stands and slightly shifts his body stage left.*]

One is younger. He's incarcerated now. That's the one I fell in love with. [*Beat.*] [*Bitterly*] And I fell because I fell for a lot of jail-bird jargon lines. [*Softer*] When summertime came and I went to visit him, the sweet nothings he would say to me. They penetrated like gosh [*making a sound effect like things whizzing by a person's head, "Phewphewphew"*]. I bought it, hook, line, and sinker. And then all these great things that we were gonna do and have and whatever when he got out. [*Bitterly*] And none of that happened. [*Beat.*] But like I said, he's young and he's not all that bright, so I understand him a lot more now but it's not enough understanding to make me even want to think about loving him.

D.C. (E. Patrick Johnson) recalls having his heart broken by an ex-con.

That's just something for others, not me. [*Sitting*] I don't want to love no guy, no gay person, period. And I guess I'll grow old and die like that.

[*Long pause.*]

[*Changing the subject*] But I was a baller back in the day. At Southern University I had numerous gay experiences. I mean plenty. In fact, there wasn't a sport that we had there that I didn't have an athlete that I was having sex with. Seriously. Serious as a heart attack. And it was all good. It was all good. [*Beat.*] I was student mascot. I traveled with the football team. There were many that were my bedmates. [*Bragging*] I mean sometimes it got a little complicated because folks would want to fight over me. If I thought about the number of athletes I had at Southern University, or just on the football team, golly . . . I'd have to be doing some counting.

I wasn't gonna say this, but in one day, I had nine athletes. And I only had the ninth one because he was supposed to be all of that. And all his buddies on the track team were daring me that I couldn't *handle* him. And so I said, "Shit, why not? One more won't hurt." And he was supposed to have me hollering, and I said, "He ain't shit." I said, [*simulating being penetrated from behind*] "That's supposed to be hurting me right there? After eight already, what can you do?" [*Realizing what he's doing*] Oh you know, that's just one of the things. It was a lot of sex going on at Southern, yes indeed.

[D.C. *sits back in his chair.*]

But you know, AIDS has taken the ultimate pleasure out of sex for me. And what I mean by that is that there's nothing better than skin-to-skin sex. It's just nothing like it. And I miss that. I went to the bathhouse a few times, and I know they still have them but because of that animal, I haven't been. It's been fifteen years or better. And that was another situation that was skin-to-skin. And I wish that they could soon find some kind of cure for the animal because the way I see it, the way that people are having sex now, especially in this town, they are not even paying attention to safe sex. They just go about their business and do it. It's like, "Well, if I get burned, I'm burned." We lost a lot of people in our club to AIDS.

[*Beat.*]

But the thing about it is, it's more young people who've gone than otherwise. And to me the young people just don't think, they don't care, they just go and they do, you know. But the majority of those young people that I'm talking about were people that were from here who went to Atlanta and got the bug and came home to die. Yeah. If I hear somebody say they're coming back from Atlanta, I start setting my watch to see how long they're going to be around, because that's been the pattern. They're not coming to slow little Baton Rouge just because they love Mama Dearest or Daddy Dearest, or home cooking, or whatever. That's not the reason. They're coming home because they're sick and they're going to need somebody to take care of them.

[D.C. *exits and* R. DIONEAUX *enters as if marching off to war, pacing frantically downstage back and forth.*]

[Projection: "R. Dioneaux—Florida Panhandle"]

R. DIONEAUX [*rapid-fire*]: I think it's a *sin* for the black church not to have an AIDS ministry since the cases of AIDS are so high in our community. It is a sin. Everybody wanna talk about Christ and deities and all that. But I happen to have read that book—that sixty-six volume book a few times. Yes, I actually read it. It doesn't just sit on a desk and collect dust and have everybody's birth certificates in it. I actually read it. And I remember that deity said, "Feed my sheep. If you love me, feed my sheep. Take care of my sheep." It also said in Matthew 25:40, "Whatsoever you do to the least of these, you do unto Me." So that person that singing in the choir that might have purple spots in two years or three years later, is still a part of—not *a parti*—but a part of the African American community. And we are going to have to be very honest. I mean we can't even call it AIDS. [*Mockingly*] We call it "the ninja." Or they'll say, "Oooh, he's siiiick. He's siiiiiiiick." And you can tell by the voice inflection, like you know what it is. I mean I'm almost waiting for somebody to say, "He has R-O-L-A-I-D-S." I'm *waiting* for that to come out, but I mean that is what we have here. A lot of dishonesty.

But, let's go back. It's racist because we assume only African American men are down low brothers. That they're the only ones that are cheating on women with other men. That's racist and stupid. Obviously, it can't be just black men with all the white men who want big black dick. Obviously, *that's not the case!* But it's also sexist because we assume that women do not marry to hide their sexual identity. [*Pausing to growl*] And as far as the issue of HIV, I cannot tell you how many sisters have told brothers, "Why you wearing a condom? You must be a punk." Take ownership. You want to talk about why I can't trust this man? My worldview is, assume everybody's HIV-positive and conduct yourself accordingly. Conduct. Yourself. Accordingly. I mean, nobody's telling you not to use condoms. "Well, he doesn't act as this way." Well, why would he? You're going to ostracize this person if they do this or that, so they do exactly as you say. [*Mockingly*] "Well we don't mind you being gay, just don't be the flaming guy." So you give them what they want. And you're mad about it? I mean you're the lie that the liar produced. You want the truth, then you start the truth at the beginning. Don't get mad that the person evolved into the lie that you told them to produce. If you don't want a dog, don't raise a puppy.

[R. DIONEAUX *does one last scan of the audience before exiting, then blackout.* EPJ *sings "Wade in the Water."*]

Wade in the water
Wade in the water, children
Wade in the water
God's gonna trouble the water

[Projection: "EPJ"]

[*Lights rise on* EPJ *at the trunk performing a ritual on the lid with* R. DIONEAUX's *dashiki, bead necklaces, and a candle. The dashiki should be draped on top of the lid first to provide a base for the candle. If using a real candle,* EPJ *lights it with a match or lighter; if using a battery-operated candle, he turns it on before speaking.*]

EPJ: I didn't make it to Reggie's funeral.

[EPJ *places a necklace around the candle, the first of four that together should create a cross, when viewed from above.*]

Or, I should say, I chose not to go. I don't do death well. Never have. Some of the most traumatic memories I have are of attending funerals—Uncle Jake's, Uncle Boot's, Aunt Mary Lee's, Uncle Johnny's, Grandmama's. Death is the one thing that I'm most frightened of, but also the one thing that I know I'll never escape. And when I began to lose some of my closet friends to AIDS, I couldn't deal.

[*Placing a necklace around the candle*] I didn't make it to Reggie's funeral. After he was hospitalized, Stacie would call or Buster would call or Kent would call—they would all call to update me on how he was doing. "He smiled today." "He's lost a lot of weight." "He's in good spirits." "He slept the whole time I was there." We were all in denial about what we knew was coming. We kept clinging to Reggie's resilience. He was always getting himself into *something*. And he always managed to get himself out. Not this time.

[*Placing a necklace around the candle*] I didn't make it to Reggie's funeral. We sang next to each other in the gospel choir in college. He was not a very strong singer, but he loved to sing. And somehow that's all that mattered. I envied his audacity to be true to himself, to embrace all of who he was, including his gayness in the midst of the shame and stigma on our campus. But when he became infected, I became angry. He was there when we heard about this disease in 1986, our sophomore year. He was there when Tom died, when David Michael died, when Sam died. He was there. And now he's gone.

[*Placing a necklace around the candle*] I didn't make it to Reggie's funeral. And I haven't made it to the eleven others since.

[EPJ *blows out the candle (or turns it off) and sets it on the floor, folds up the dashiki with the beads, and places the candle and folded dashiki inside the trunk. He sings the last line of the song while closing the lid of the trunk.*]

God's gonna trouble the water . . .

[*Slow fade to black.* CHAZ/CHASTITY *enters, wearing dramatic earrings and a feather boa.*]

[Projection: "Chaz/Chastity—Hickory, North Carolina"]

CHAZ/CHASTITY: For the longest time, I always knew that there was something different about me. I knew that when I would disrobe, that I was, quote unquote, a male. My mother never hesitated to remind me that she had two sons, but I was always very effeminate in my nature.

A sexual therapist diagnosed me as a pre-operative transsexual, saying that I had more female chromosomes in my anatomy than male, and that through medication and surgery, he could make my body match the way that my mind was. But part of that process was that you were to be subjected to living as a female, or to live out the gender reassignment for at least a year, the minimum of a year, and during that time you were evaluated mentally, physically, and emotionally, to make sure that you were truly transgender. I did that for five years. For five years I worked, lived, slept, breathed, ate, as a female here in Hickory.

[*Preening as if on a runaway*] Here is this five-foot-eleven "woman," very statuesque, large feet, large hands, but very immaculately dressed and very polished. It was just almost too good to be true. No natural woman would look that good and pay that particular amount of attention to detail.

After five years, during the course of that time, I had a really bad dream one night. And in the dream, I saw this SUV pull up into my driveway, and out of the SUV stepped my brother. Well, no sooner than he stepped out of the SUV, there were like hundreds of people who surrounded him, and they brutally beat him to death, in my driveway. In the dream, I recall running to my mother and to my father to try to awake them from their sleep but they would not awaken. I went to the doors and to the windows, beating, pounding upon them, and it was to no avail; I could not get them to open. I recall awaking from the dream and my hand was still on the telephone's receiver, where I was evidently trying to dial nine-one-one for help, because my brother was lying there, on my driveway in a pool of blood, and there was nothing I could do to save him. And so, the dream shook me up so bad, and it was so intense, that I could not go back to sleep. A very dear friend of mine at the time was Glenda, and she was, quote unquote, "very spiritual," and in the church. She was saved, and she would always witness to me when she came to get her hair done. And so, upon me telling her the dream . . . I couldn't even get the dream out without weeping just profusely, because it was really, really horrifying. And Glenda did nothing but sit there the whole time, very quietly, a lot like you are now, and just listening very intently to every syllable that I was saying. And then I asked her did she know what the dream represented, or what it meant? And she convinced me that the dream was not my brother in actuality, but that it was me, and that the people that were kicking and beating him so profusely in the dream were not people, but actually, my inner demons. And that it was just a matter of time before something very, very violent or terrible would happen, and that God was asking me to allow Him to shield me from that.

She was going to noonday prayer that day. I said, "Well, when you go to pray, would you remember me and my family in prayer?" Well, she said that the Lord directed her to pray for me before she left. And in doing so, this overwhelming feeling came over me, and I accepted Christ, right there in my kitchen. [*Takes off boa and earrings*] Well, I went through with that, and Glenda was my mentor, and I was living life through her eyes. I was trying to appease her and appease my family, because my mother was just happy that I was no longer wearing dresses. She was happy that people were no longer talking about her son, the one that wore the dresses, and that thought he was a woman.

And what has brought me to the decision not to have the surgery was because I felt that once the doctors would have done the reassignment, meaning the physical reconstructing of my body, the only thing that they would not have been able to tamper with was my essence, who I am as a person. [*Puts boa and earrings back on*] Yes, Charles would have been no more, but "Chastity" has always been and always will be. "Chastity," I do believe, was here before Charles was. And the one thing that the surgery would not have changed was that very fact. And why should I risk losing my life on a surgeon's table to appease others? And would it truly have appeased them? Like I said, I had to become comfortable with the skin that I was in, and realizing and knowing that a physical change was not going to change who I was mentally. It may soften the blow for you to say, "Well, shit, at least she looks like a woman now. She's got natural looking breasts, and she's got a vagina, and she has soft smooth skin, or long flowing hair." But does that truly constitute being a woman? Or does a penis and facial hair and a muscular build or physique truly constitute masculinity? And the only one that can decide that is yourself. So, I can be whomever I choose to be. I can put on the most elaborate ball gowns, the most coiffed coiffures, and be every bit of Chastity that I dare to be, but it doesn't change the fact of who I am to Him.

His greatest commandment was that we love one another, but you can't love someone else until you first learn to love yourself. And being that I've embraced that, it's allowed me to embrace my effeminate nature. And the character that I'd most like to impersonate is Patti Labelle. A future goal of mine is to possibly one day land a job working at La Cage, and I think that that would be a great honor, to be able to perform before Patti. And my favorite song of hers to perform is "You Are My Friend."

[CHAZ/CHASTITY *does a lip sync routine to last few bars of "You Are My Friend" and exits.*]

[HAROLD *enters, wearing a cardigan and eyeglasses with big frames, and holding a tin of old-fashioned candies.*]

[Projection: "Harold—Washington, D.C."]

HAROLD: Forty-nine years ago, I met my partner. My partner went home with me to St. Louis for holidays, Christmas mainly. And by the way, his first name is Harold also. He's from Pennsylvania. And I have to tell you that my partner is white. And there was no conflict until my sister tried to serve him chitlins.

[HAROLD *offers random audience members candy from his tin.*]

We met in Providence, Rhode Island, where I lived. And it was the summer of 1965. A mutual friend of ours was coming to visit and he said, "Can I bring a friend? I think you'll like him." And he brought him. And I did. We ended summer vacation and corresponded until Christmas of '65. I went home to St. Louis for Christmas and I cut that short out there and stopped here in Washington, where he lived. And we spent some more time together. By the time January rolls around, I can't live without him. So I moved to Washington, D.C., and we decided that we would buy a house. It was a mostly white neighborhood. When we first moved to this house, we'd be walking and the police would follow us. One time, I got off the bus at the corner to come home, and the police was parked there and they called me over and they said, "Show me some I.D. What are you doing up here?" And I said, "I live in this block." And he said, "You live in this block?" And I said, "Yes." So, I take out my I.D. that has my address. And he did not believe me, and he walked with me until I got to the house, put the key in the door, and I said, "See ya."

[HAROLD *sits in the chair.*]

Then within our own group, the gay population, many were a little unsettled because of the interracial thing. And this is a unique thing about Washington, D.C., because it has a large African American population. So, I had more black friends than white, and it was basically African Americans that gave me flack. I remember someone telling me, "Oh, I didn't know you dealt in snow." And I had no idea what the hell he was talking about, okay? I loved my partner from the very beginning. I didn't know it would last this long. I trust him emphatically. I think he knows more of my weaknesses and accepts them more than anybody. And I didn't find that with anybody else, whatever their color may have been or their religious beliefs. What is left of relatives and friends is still a warmth and they consider us for who we are. Not what they think we are.

[HAROLD *exits as* EPJ *crosses to center stage, singing a bluesy tune.*]

EPJ: *Somebody's nibbling on somebody's neck while shuckin' corn. Ah oop!*

[Projection: "EPJ"]

EPJ: Loving across the color line has never been easy. *Loving versus Virginia.* 1967. The year I was born. Isn't it ironic? Before I met Stephen, my sweet tea, I could have argued on behalf of the state of Virginia: I went through a very militant phase after my first boyfriend, a white man. After him, I vowed *never* to date across the color line again. Never say never.

[EPJ *sits on the trunk.*]

I dated some freaky flakes and some flaky freaks. This first white boyfriend I dated dumped me because he said I smelled different. Crossing the color line was like spinning pirouettes on a razor's edge, so I retreated into blackness—that is, until Mr. Sweet Tea came along.

[*Singing*] *Somebody's whispering sweet nothings in somebody's ear while sipping tea. Ahh oop!*

We met online. AOL. Y'all remember back in the day? He was a chat buddy of a good friend of mine. They met in the white4black chat room—a room I had vowed to stay out of—because it didn't quite *smell* right. His screen name was SCWHT4BLK. South Carolina White For Black. Given my last experience, that screen name said RUN. That was July 1998 and in October of that same year we met in person at my place in Durham. I cooked dinner. We walked the dog. We danced. We had dessert. We had *dessert*. The next morning my series of questions began: "So, what was this? Was this just a fuck? Are you interested in seeing me again? Whichever it is, I'm cool. I just want to know," I lied. He decided that he would see me again and we would see how it went. The first few months were interesting. We learned a lot. He learned that you can't refer to black people as spades—even in innocent jest. And I learned that "poor white trash" is what I grew up as, only in blackface. He accepted his white privilege in the face of my bouginess, and I released the guilt about dating a white man who dared to love me across the color line.

[EPJ *reprises the song and vamps, getting the audience to sing "ah oop"
in blues rhythm while he riffs.*]

   Somebody's nibbling, and shucking, and whispering . . .

[EPJ *repeats as so moved; ends audience singing.*]

   While loving me, my Stephen. Ah oop!

[*Montage of characters' names over a drone sound and drumming can
be heard.* EPJ *goes to the altar and picks up the tea service and the container with the sugar and places them on top of the trunk. He then
walks to the side table and gets the mason jar of unsweetened tea and
walks back to the trunk and places it on the top of the trunk. He un-
screws the lid of the mason jar filled with tea and places the lid beside
the jar; he then picks up the container with the mixed sugars and holds
it horizontally and rocks it back and forth to mix them.*]

EPJ [*still mixing the sugars in the jar*]: These stories dance at the zenith
   of dusk and dawn, spinning new tales in the light of the moon and
   sun.

[EPJ *puts the container down, takes the lid off, and uses the attached
scooper to gather some sugar and pours it into the mason jar of tea.
He picks the jar up and, while holding the jar between both hands, he
makes a circular motion with it as he speaks.*]

   They are my brothers' stories, father's stories, sons' stories, granddaddy's stories, great granddaddy's stories, and the stories from
   as far back as my mind's eye can imagine. They are my elixir for
   living inside my own truth, my tea.

[EPJ *takes a long sip of tea from the mason jar.*]

Sweet and bitter.

[*He twists the lid back on the jar.*]

It's the will to tell the story that's important.

[EPJ *holds the jar up as if toasting. Either an image of* COUNTESS VIVIAN *is projected on the screen or the actor playing* COUNTESS VIVIAN *returns to upstage right, dimly lit. A beat, and then fade to black.*]